MARTY KOEPKE

Between the Clicks

The Hidden Work of Healthcare Informatics

First published by Platypus Publishing 2025

First edition

ISBN: 978-1-965016-73-2

This book was professionally typeset on Reedsy.
Find out more at reedsy.com

Contents

Prologue

This book is for anyone who's just starting out in healthcare informatics profession (using the most general term "informaticist", in the career field of "informatics") —or anyone curious about what this field is really about. If you're feeling overwhelmed or unsure about how to take the next step, you're in the right place. I've been there. I know what it feels like to walk into a room and not know what you're supposed to do next.

I didn't start in this field with a grand plan. My journey was messy, full of unexpected opportunities and lessons learned the hard way. But every experience taught me something valuable. This book is built on those lessons—real-world stories, practical tips, and advice for growing your skills.

You won't find long-winded theory here. This book is about what works in real life. By the end, you'll know how to see the big picture, ask the right questions, and gain critical skills to help facilitate effective design solutions that actually make life easier for clinicians and patients.

You'll also explore the many roles you'll take on as an informaticist —**Observer, Translator, Facilitator, Advocate, Liaison, Designer, Change Manager, Student**. Each role will challenge you in different ways. Some days, you'll wear several hats at once. That's okay. You'll learn how to juggle them, just like I did.

Informatics is about solving real problems. It's about connecting the dots between clinical needs and technical solutions. It's about staying curious, learning from every experience, and leaning on others along the way.

This isn't just a job—it's a chance to make a difference. By the time you finish this book, its my hope you'll have the mindset, and confidence to do just that.

Introduction

I never planned to work in healthcare. Honestly, it was just practical. I had two young kids at home, and working evenings and weekends at the hospital let me be with them during the day. My job as a unit clerk and monitor tech in the ICU was steady, flexible, and gave me a front-row seat to how things worked in healthcare. I didn't have a master plan back then. It was just a job that fit my life.

Over time, something shifted. I started to enjoy the rhythm of healthcare. I got curious—about how clinicians worked, how information flowed, and how all the moving parts of a healthcare organization. That curiosity pushed me to pursue my Master's in Healthcare Administration. It seemed like the next logical step, though I still didn't know exactly where it would lead.

Then came the opportunity that changed everything. The hospital was preparing for a major EHR upgrade, and I was asked to help document current state workflows. I didn't know what that even meant at first. I spent hours shadowing clinicians, trying to piece together how things actually worked. Soon, I was helping evaluate provider note templates and preparing them for the new system. I even got sent for EHR build training—a big step that felt like a leap into something unknown.

But life has its twists. The hospital underwent some changes, and it became clear I needed a new direction. When the CNIO suggested I look for a career in informatics, I laughed. Informatics? No way. That didn't sound like me at all. But then... I saw a job posting for an EHR analyst role. It paid a little more, and I figured I had enough experience to give it a shot.

I wasn't looking for a career in informatics, but that's exactly what I found.

The first few months were overwhelming. I had to figure out how to design workflows, coordinate changes, build solutions, plan upgrades, and train staff. I knew just enough to get started, but the real learning came from mentors—providers and leaders—who invested their time in me. They taught me how to observe, think critically, approach problems with curiosity, and focus on what really matters: building solutions that improve patient care, and make their lives easier.

Every step in my journey was shaped by the people who came alongside me. Without them, I wouldn't have grown into each new role. Now, it's my turn to give back—to help the next generation of healthcare informatics professionals step into this world with confidence and curiosity, just like others helped me.

Let's get started.

1

The Many Hats of the Informaticist

When I stepped into my first role as an EHR analyst, I assumed my job was to build and support the system. What I didn't realize was that healthcare informatics isn't just about technology—it's about people, workflows, and change. I wasn't just a builder or a troubleshooter. I became a problem-solver, facilitator, translator, teacher, and more.

Each task I took on introduced a new role. Observing workflows meant stepping into The Observer role—seeing the reality of clinical work beyond the system's design. Translating clinical needs into system requirements turned me into The Translator, ensuring IT could build solutions that made sense for users. When I started designing better workflows, I became The Designer, balancing usability, compliance, and efficiency.

Many people ask, "What does an informaticist actually do?" The answer is, a little bit of everything. We onboard new staff, manage EHR upgrades, handle requests, and integrate new technology into clinical workflows. But more than that, we move between roles based on the situation. One moment, you're a Liaison connecting teams. The next, you're a Change Manager helping people adopt a new process.

Informatics isn't a single role—it's the ability to wear the right hat at the right time. Some days, you'll juggle multiple roles at once. That's the challenge—but it's also what makes this work exciting.

Let me introduce you to the key roles you'll take on in this field. Each will push you to grow in new ways, shaping you into an informaticist who can connect dots, solve problems, and build solutions that truly make a difference.

The Observer: Seeing the Whole Picture Through Workflow Analysis

Observation is where informatics begins. Before you can fix a workflow or design a solution, you must first understand how things actually work—not just how they are supposed to work. That means watching, listening, and asking the right questions before jumping to conclusions.

When I first started, I assumed I could spot inefficiencies quickly. But real insights come when you step back, observe without interference, and look for patterns. A process might seem smooth on the surface, but the hidden problems are often in the extra steps, unnecessary clicks, or small frustrations that build up over time.

The best observers don't just document workflows—they trace data movement, analyze process gaps, and validate findings with users.

The Translator: Bridging Clinical Needs and Technical Solutions

Once you've observed a workflow, your next role is to become a translator—bridging the gap between clinical needs and technical solutions. If no one connects these worlds, miscommunication leads to poor system design and frustrated users.

Being a translator isn't just about taking requests and passing them to IT. It's about digging deeper, asking the right questions, and ensuring both sides truly understand each other. Early in my career, I assumed what providers asked for was exactly what they needed. I quickly learned that without deeper exploration, the solution rarely solves the real problem.

The best translators simplify complexity, remove jargon, and bring teams together.

The Advocate: Prioritizing User-Friendly, Patient-Centered Designs While Being Compliance-Aware

One of the most important roles you'll take on as an informaticist is being an advocate. Your job isn't just to build what clinicians request or what IT says is possible—it's to champion solutions that enhance patient care, improve usability, and remain compliant with regulations.

Early in my career, I thought advocacy meant making things easier for clinicians. That's part of it, but it's only the beginning. True advocacy means seeing the bigger picture—understanding how workflows, documentation, and system design impact patient care, regulatory requirements, and long-term usability.

One of my biggest lessons came during an EHR integration project, where we were merging ambulatory and acute workflows into a single EHR. The acute-care documentation model wasn't designed for ambulatory clinics—if left unchanged, it would have slowed providers down, fragmented patient data, and disrupted continuity of care. It took persistent conversations and reframing the issue to help acute-care leaders see the impact from the ambulatory and patient perspective. Once they saw how the disconnects affected the patient journey, everything clicked.

Being an advocate means balancing innovation, usability, and compliance.

The Facilitator: Leading Effective Meetings and Driving Decisions

Facilitating meetings might sound simple, but it's one of the most critical and challenging roles you'll take on as an informaticist. It's not just about running meetings or setting agendas—it's about guiding discussions, balancing perspectives, and ensuring clear decisions move projects forward.

At first, I thought facilitation meant leading every conversation and driving decisions. But I quickly learned that forcing a decision isn't the same as achieving consensus. Effective facilitation requires preparation, neutrality, and structured discussions to ensure that everyone's voice is heard while keeping the conversation on track.

A great facilitator creates space for collaboration, encourages engagement, and ensures meetings lead to real outcomes.

The Liaison: Connecting Teams and Breaking Down Silos

Healthcare is full of silos—clinical teams focus on patient care, IT on system stability, operations on efficiency, and compliance on regulations. While they all work toward the same goal, their day-to-day priorities often conflict. That's where the liaison role comes in.

As a liaison, your job is to bridge these gaps, ensure teams communicate effectively, and prevent costly misalignment. I learned just how critical this role was during a referral management project across multiple healthcare markets. Each market had a different referral process—some centralized, others decentralized. My task wasn't just to build a solution; it was to bring all stakeholders together, find common ground, and ensure that the final workflow worked across the organization.

The key to being an effective liaison is building relationships and trust.

When teams trust you, they are more open to collaboration, and aligning perspectives becomes easier. Sometimes, the most valuable thing you can do is remind teams why they're working together and keep the big picture in focus.

The Designer: Building Practical, Real-World Solutions

Designing solutions is where everything starts to come together. After observing workflows and translating needs, it's time to create something that works in real life—not just in theory.

Healthcare informatics isn't about building the most advanced or technically impressive system—it's about creating solutions that clinicians can actually use. A well-designed solution fits naturally into workflows, improves efficiency, and enhances patient care without unnecessary complexity.

I've learned to start with the basics. Keep the design simple, test it, and iterate before adding layers of complexity. Think of it like building a house—you lay a strong foundation before adding walls and a roof. The best solutions aren't created in isolation—they come from collaboration, testing, and refinement. No design is perfect the first time, and less is often more when it comes to usability.

The Change Manager: Managing Change and User Adoption

Informatics is full of ideas, complaints, and requests for change. Some come from frontline staff seeking efficiency, others from regulatory mandates or leadership initiatives. But one of the biggest lessons I've learned is that not every request should move forward—change must be evaluated, prioritized, and structured before implementation.

This is where governance comes in.

Good governance isn't just a formality—it's a safeguard. It ensures that changes are necessary, well-designed, and aligned with strategic priorities. Governance starts long before a formal review, in the pre-governance phase, when we define the problem, seek leadership sponsorship, and determine whether a request is even needed.

Not every issue requires a system build, and not every request is a priority. Leadership plays a key role in deciding what aligns with broader goals and how it fits with other projects.

Once a request is validated and designed, it should never be pushed to build without structured review and approval. Poorly vetted changes can disrupt workflows, introduce compliance risks, and create more problems than they solve.

As an informaticist, you're not the decision-maker, but you are a steward of the change process. You help guide governance, engage the right people, and ensure changes move forward the right way.

The Student: Embracing Continuous Learning and Adaptability

Informatics is constantly evolving. New technologies, workflows, and challenges will push you to keep learning and adapting. You'll never have all the answers, and that's okay. What matters is that you stay curious, ask the right questions, and keep growing.

Early in my career, I assumed that experience would eventually lead to mastery—that if I learned enough, I'd eventually know everything I needed to succeed. But over time, I realized that the best health informatics professionals aren't the ones who have all the answers—they're the ones who keep asking questions.

Some of the biggest mistakes in informatics happen when people assume they already know the right answer. The way something worked last year may not be how it works today. A system upgrade, a regulatory change, or a workflow shift can introduce unexpected challenges. The only way to stay ahead is to approach every situation with fresh eyes.

Being a student means getting comfortable with not knowing everything. It means shadowing roles you've never done, sitting in on meetings you don't fully understand, and always being willing to ask, "Why?"

Bringing It All Together

Informatics is about wearing many hats and knowing when to switch between them. Some days, you'll be an observer, watching workflows unfold and identifying gaps. Other days, you'll be deep in design, building a practical solution, or guiding a team through change. No two days will be the same, and that's what makes this work so rewarding.

These roles aren't just things you'll do—they'll shape who you become as a professional. They'll challenge you, push you, and teach you how to think bigger and collaborate better.

In the chapters that follow, we'll dive deeper into each role, giving you the tools and practical steps you need to grow in each one. This isn't about being perfect from the start. It's about learning, adapting, and becoming the kind of informaticist who can make a real difference.

Let's begin.

2

The Observer—Seeing the Whole Picture

The first role you'll take on as an informaticist is that of The Observer. Observation is where everything begins. You can't improve a workflow, design a solution, or make a system better unless you fully understand how things work right now. That means watching, listening, and asking the right questions—not jumping to conclusions or rushing to fix things. Observation is about seeing the whole picture, and it lays the foundation for everything that follows.

In my early days, I didn't even realize I was playing this role. My first taste of informatics was helping document current state workflows during an EHR upgrade at the hospital. I was asked to shadow providers, nurses, and unit coordinators, capturing how they worked and documenting every step. The real work began, however, when I became an analyst. That's when I realized that observation isn't passive—it's an active process.

At first, I thought my job was just to watch and take notes, but that only got me so far. The real insights came when I started asking questions:

- Why are you doing it that way?
- Why in that order?

- What's slowing you down, and what do you do to work around it?

Those questions opened doors. The more I asked, the more I saw how things fit together—or didn't. Each session left me with a new set of questions:

- Is there a better way to do this?
- Could this step be simpler?
- Why isn't the system supporting this process better?

I would take those questions back with me and practice on my own, testing workflows, experimenting with new ideas, and trying to connect the dots. That combination of curiosity, analysis, and hands-on practice taught me more than any formal training ever could.

Where I Struggled

When I first started observing workflows, I struggled to balance watching and acting. I felt pressure to offer quick solutions, but that often led to assumptions or missed details. I'd notice something that seemed like a problem and jump in to "fix" it, only to realize later that I hadn't seen the full picture.

It was also awkward to just stand there, especially when clinicians were busy. I worried I was getting in the way. The more uncomfortable I felt, the more tempted I was to rush through the observation.

What I Learned

Slow Down and Observe Fully:

I learned to resist the urge to offer solutions right away. Taking time to see the whole workflow helped me avoid mistakes and find deeper insights.

Ask Open-Ended Questions:

Instead of asking yes/no questions, I started asking broader questions like "What's the most frustrating part of this workflow?" or "What would make this process easier?" These questions led to richer answers and new perspectives.

Embrace the Awkwardness:

Over time, I realized that standing quietly and observing was part of the job. Once I explained why I was there, most clinicians were happy to let me watch and even pointed out things I might have missed.

Observation is Active, Not Passive

Sometimes, the real problems hide in plain sight. It might be something small—a nurse taking extra steps to grab a supply or a provider needing to click through multiple screens just to complete a basic task. These small inefficiencies might seem harmless, but they add up quickly. If you're not paying attention, you'll miss them.

Being an observer is an active, intentional process. You have to stay curious and keep asking questions, even when it feels uncomfortable. The key isn't just documenting every step of a workflow—it's understanding the story behind each step. Why does this process exist? How did it evolve? What purpose does each action serve, and could it be done differently?

One of the most valuable skills you'll develop is the ability to ask deeper, more meaningful questions:

- When does this process break down? Why?
- What's the workaround, and why did it become necessary?
- How does this process change depending on the setting or situation?

It took me a while, but I finally learned that silence is powerful. When you ask a question, give people time to think and respond. The pause might feel awkward, but trust me—that's often when the most honest and valuable answers come out. If you jump in too quickly with ideas or solutions, you'll miss the deeper insights hiding beneath the surface.

Seeing Patterns and Gaps

The more you observe, the more patterns will start to emerge. You'll notice what's working, where things slow down, and where workflows fall apart. Informatics is all about finding those gaps and connecting the dots.

Sometimes, the solution is simple—combining two steps into one, or leveraging an available filter. Other times, it's more complex, requiring a full redesign of the process. Either way, your job as an observer is to bring those gaps to the surface and understand why they exist.

I remember a project where I was asked to help map out the workflow for health maintenance. At first, it seemed like a straightforward process: Go to the health maintenance module, and document the screening measure that was completed. Indicate when it is next due. Easy peasy, right? Not so much! It turns out that each clinical quality measure has unique nuances. The module didn't account for these things. Every step was manual, and it took staff so long to update everything, it wasn't used reliably. In order to work, it had to be optimized.

Taking the time to first listen to the user's needs and then compare that against their actual technology experience is one of the most powerful things you can do as an observer. It's not just about what's happening in front of you—it's about following the data.

Ask yourself:

- Where does the information come from?
- Where does the information go after this step?
- Does it reach the right person or system?
- What manual steps are required along the way?
- Where are their gaps between what the users need and what the technology does?

These small details matter. They're the difference between a seamless process and a broken one.

Collaboration is Key

Observation doesn't end with you. Once you've mapped out what's happening, take your observations back to the people living the workflow every day. Walk them through what you've seen and ask if it matches their experience. This feedback loop is critical.

In one project, I mapped out a clinic's patient intake process and thought I had nailed it. But when I brought it back to the back office staff, they pointed out steps I hadn't noticed—steps that made all the difference. The best insights come from collaboration. Always validate your observations with the people who know the process best.

The Foundation for Every Other Role

Being an observer isn't just the first role you'll take on—it's the foundation for every other role you'll play as an informaticist. Every great design starts with great observation. Every successful change begins with fully understanding what needs to be changed.

When you take the time to truly see the full picture, you set yourself up for success in every role that follows—whether you're translating needs, designing solutions, managing change, or advocating for better workflows.

In the next chapter, we'll dive into the Translator role—where observation meets action. This is where you'll learn how to take everything you've seen and turn it into something that both technical and clinical teams can actually leverage.

Let's keep going.

Practical Tips

Focus on transitions:

- Most workflow issues happen when information passes from one person or system to another.

Trace the data:

- Following the flow of information through the system is just as important as observing physical workflows.

Involve clinicians early:

- Reviewing your findings with them helps validate your observations and builds trust.

3

The Translator—Bridging The Gap

One of the most critical roles you'll take on as an informaticist is The Translator. You're the bridge between two very different worlds—clinical teams who live in workflows and patient care and technical teams who speak in system configurations, data flows, and system requirements. Without someone in the middle translating these needs, things can break down quickly.

Requests that sound simple on the surface—"Make this faster," "Can the orders come back automatically?"—are rarely straightforward. A clinician might know what they want, but not how to explain it in technical terms. Analysts may have the technical expertise, but they don't live in the day-to-day clinical workflow and often don't see how the problem manifests in real time. Your role as a translator is to bridge that gap and ensure both sides truly understand each other.

Your job isn't to pass the request along. It's to dig deeper and understand the root of the problem. Why does the process feel slow? What steps are causing delays? What outcome are they ultimately hoping for? Once you've uncovered the true need, you can turn it into clear, actionable requirements that IT can build—solutions that work for clinicians, patients, and the organization as a whole.

Where I Struggled

When I first started in this field, I struggled to fully understand the problem before offering solutions. Providers would explain what they needed, and I didn't know how to convert that into a holistic solution. I needed more specific details to help convert a user request into a technical solution.

The result? Solutions that didn't work or didn't fully solve the underlying problem. We'd implement something only to have to revisit it later because we hadn't addressed the root cause, or the create a complete design.

Once I started working with other technical teams, it became more obvious that each group spoke a different language. Clinical teams described their needs in broad, workflow-based terms, while analysts needed precise technical details. Bridging that gap took time—and a lot of trial and error.

What I Learned

Document, Document, Document:

- Write out all the steps and hand-offs for the current state.
- Clearly highlight where issues or needs are.
- Make sure it is in plain language that everyone can understand.
- Write out the proposed solution as simply as you can, with as much detail as you can.

Ask "Why" at Least Three Times:

- As you are documenting, dig deeper into every step to uncover the real problem.
- The root of every problem leads back to either people, process or platform issues.

Summarize and Re-frame:

- Repeating what you've heard back to the clinician, and even to IT helps ensure that everyone is on the same page and gain consensus that everyone understands what needs to be solved and the plan to do so.
- This simple step saves a lot of time and confusion later.

Translating Through Hands-On Exploration

Listening isn't enough. Once you've gathered information from providers and observed their workflows, it's time to take the next step; dig into the system and recreate the workflow, click by click. This is where the magic happens.

Go into a lower non-production domain or use test patients and walk through the workflow as if you were the clinician. Pay attention to every step. Test how the system behaves at each point. Where does the process break down? What do you see that the user may not have noticed? This hands-on testing will confirm what they're experiencing—or reveal something different entirely.

In one project, medical assistants were frustrated with how long it took to locate needed documentation for pre-visit planning. After listening to their concerns, I recreated the process in a test environment. Click by click, I examined their viewpoints. That's when I noticed a set of filters that had been sitting there all along. These filters weren't activated for their workflow, but it could reduce their preparation time by half.

This type of hands-on exploration is critical for understanding the 'nitty-gritty' of how the system works. Sometimes, it shows you that the problem is easily fixable. Other times, it exposes a true system gap that requires a bigger solution. Either way, it gives you the evidence you need to translate more effectively when working with IT.

Turning Needs into Requirements

Now that you've listened, observed, and tested, it's time to turn what you've learned into clear technical requirements. This is where translating becomes more of an art than a science.

Clinical teams often describe needs in broad terms—"Make this easier" or "Streamline the order process."

IT, however, needs specifics:

- What should the system do?
- What triggers the action?
- What data needs to flow, where and when?

In my early days, someone would come to me with a request to create a new electronic form for documentation. The request often seemed simple at first—"We need a new form with these fields for providers to fill out." My role was to mock up the form with all the required fields and submit it for approval. But once it reached the analysts, the complexity started to unfold.

Questions would come back that I wasn't initially prepared for:

- "Where in the table structure do we store these fields?"
- "Should these questions appear in the chart summary, or are they just for internal documentation?"
- "Which print templates need to include these fields?"

And just when I thought I had it figured out, an analyst would raise a critical question:

- "You know, another form has nearly identical questions.
- "Should we leverage those existing fields, or do we create a new structured data field with slightly different responses?"

These weren't just technical details—they were decisions that affected data integrity, reporting, and long-term usability. As I gained more experience, I realized these details couldn't be ignored during translation. They were essential to ensuring the form worked not just on the surface, but deep within the system's structure.

While we'll explore these nuances more in the Designer role, understanding where translation is heading early on is critical. You don't need to know every answer right away, but being aware of the broader technical implications helps you become a more effective translator and prepares you for what's to come.

Simplify, Simplify, Simplify

The best translators make complex ideas simple—for both clinical teams and technical teams. No jargon. No buzzwords. Just clear, plain language that everyone can understand. Your goal is to bridge two different worlds, which means you have to tailor your message depending on who's listening.

When presenting a solution to clinical teams, you focus on workflow impact and how the change will improve their day-to-day tasks. But simplification works the other direction, too. When you're working with EHR analysts, lab analysts, or integration analysts, it's just as important to translate user needs into simple, actionable technical requirements. Technology can be black and white, and these teams work best when the design documentation is precise and unambiguous.

If your requirements are vague or overly complex, it creates confusion and slows down the build process. Strive to break everything into clear, concise steps that technical teams can act on. For example, instead of "Update lab notifications for all high-priority tests," specify exactly which tests need updating, what triggers the notification, and who the intended recipient is. Clarity saves time and reduces the risk of miscommunication.

Visuals remain one of your most powerful tools. Workflow diagrams, data flow charts, and swim lane diagrams help both clinical and technical teams stay aligned. I've seen a simple diagram resolve complex design discussions in minutes by giving everyone a shared reference point.

Ultimately, simplification is about creating shared understanding. The more you reduce complexity—whether for clinical end users or technical teams—the better the results will be for everyone involved.

Staying Connected to Both Worlds

To be an effective translator, you must stay connected to both clinical and technical teams. It's easy to get pulled toward one side, especially when you're more comfortable with clinical workflows or technical build processes. But living in only one world limits your ability to translate effectively. Clinicians rely on you to accurately represent their needs, while technical teams need you to bring context, clarity, and actionable requirements to the table.

Spending time on both sides is essential. Shadow clinicians and listen to front-line staff to understand how they interact with the system in real-world settings. Observe how workflows play out—not just in a perfect scenario, but during busy shifts or unusual cases. Then, sit with IT analysts to learn about system limitations, data flows, and how different modules interact. You'll gain a deeper appreciation for what's possible within the system and where adjustments can be made.

In one project, I was tasked with implementing a new referral module across multiple markets. The challenge was that each market had their referral management processes defined differently. In one market, there was a centralized referrals team, in another market a connection center team help manage outbound referrals, and in another region, the medical assistant had to manage the entire workflow process. One size did not fit all. In this instance, we had to get all the markets together, with myself and one of our top system architects. We spent hours listening to their needs, and translating those needs into feasible technical options. As a result of the time we spent listening and translating, we ended up designing a custom solution that would allow all the markets to leverage a single tools for their varying workflows.

Understanding both sides makes you a better translator, helping you build trust with clinicians and IT while ensuring that the solutions you deliver actually work in practice.

The Bridge Between Needs and Solutions

Being a translator is more than just a role—it's the bridge that holds everything together. When you do it well, workflows become seamless, solutions feel intuitive, and clinical teams adopt what's been built because it truly meets their needs.

The key to being an effective bridge is to stay curious and keep asking questions at every step. Even when you think you understand the problem, dig a little deeper. Test everything for yourself in a lower environment. Recreate the workflow click by click, just as the user would. This hands-on exploration gives you the insight you need to ask better questions and refine your requirements.

Simplification plays a big role here, too. Just as you simplify complex ideas for clinical teams, you also need to translate user requests into clear, detailed technical requirements for IT. Providing specifics—exact data fields, workflow triggers, and output expectations—ensures that everyone is working toward the same goal.

The more you dig into the details, the more trust you'll build with both clinicians and technical teams. You become the person they rely on to connect the dots and make complex solutions understandable.

In the next chapter, we'll explore the Facilitator role, where the insights you've gathered as a translator become the foundation for collaboration and decision-making. Your ability to guide discussions, build consensus, and align diverse perspectives will be critical in turning those translated needs into actionable next steps. This is where ideas start to take shape and consensus turns into progress.

This is just the beginning—there's more to learn.

Practical Tips

Engage a Broad Group of Stakeholders Early:

- Don't limit conversations to just IT or clinical leadership. Bring in providers, nurses, quality teams, and other relevant roles—such as lab, radiology, or pharmacy—who will be impacted by the workflow. Diverse perspectives help uncover hidden challenges and lead to more balanced solutions.

Visualize the Workflow:

- Draw it out, even if it's just a rough sketch. Seeing the process mapped out helps clarify where things are breaking down and gives everyone a shared view of the current state.

Stay Curious and Patient:

- Translating takes practice and persistence. Be willing to ask questions, listen carefully, and seek clarification until you understand the full picture. Every conversation helps you get closer to a solution that truly works.

4

The Facilitator– Gaining Consensus

Facilitation is one of the hardest, but most valuable, skills you'll develop as an informaticist. It's not just about running meetings or setting agendas—it's about guiding discussions, balancing personalities, and helping teams reach clear decisions that move projects forward.

At first, I thought facilitation meant leading the conversation—steering the discussion and making sure decisions happened. But I quickly learned that true facilitation isn't about control—it's about creating structure, keeping people focused, and making sure every voice is heard.

It builds directly on your skills as a translator. Once you've gathered insights from clinicians and turned them into clear requirements, the next step is to bring stakeholders into the conversation and help them align on a shared solution. This is where great ideas take shape and turn into action.

But without structure, meetings can spiral into chaos—dominated by a few voices, full of side conversations, and ultimately unproductive. As the facilitator, your job is to keep discussions on track, ask the right questions, and create a space where teams can reach meaningful decisions.

Where I Struggled

I struggled with all of it! I rarely created agendas in advance, which meant meetings often lacked clear objectives. Conversations would wander, and I had trouble keeping people on task without shutting down valuable input. Strong personalities—whether it was someone dominating the conversation or someone staying silent despite having critical insights—were difficult to balance.

Scope creep was another challenge. Discussions would start with a specific issue but quickly expand into unrelated topics, making it hard to wrap up the meeting with a clear decision. And even when a meeting felt productive, I'd often forget to document follow-ups and action items, which meant nothing actually moved forward.

Facilitation is a real skill, and I had to actively work to develop it over time.

What I Learned

Facilitators create space for others, not just themselves:

Instead of trying to drive decisions, I learned to ask the right questions, listen carefully, and ensure the conversation stays balanced.

Structure is everything:

Without a clear agenda, defined objectives, and time management, meetings easily become unproductive. Planning in advance sets the entire conversation up for success.

Documentation matters:

No matter how good a meeting is, if action items and decisions aren't captured, it's as if the conversation never happened.

Managing personalities takes strategy:

Instead of trying to control strong voices, I learned to redirect discussions back to the agenda, and instead of letting quiet participants fade into the background, I started calling on them directly.

Preparing for Success

Facilitation starts long before the meeting begins. The more prepared you are, the smoother the discussion will go.

Set the foundation early:

- Define the purpose of the meeting: What decision needs to be made?
- Send out an agenda ahead of time so participants come prepared.
- Identify key stakeholders and make sure the right people are in the room.

One of the most valuable things I've learned is to prepare open-ended questions in advance to keep discussions productive:

- "What are the biggest challenges in this workflow?"
- "How would this change impact patient care?"
- "What are the risks or barriers to implementing this solution?"

When meetings lack a clear purpose, people check out. But when participants understand the goal from the start, discussions become more focused and productive.

Guiding the Conversation

Facilitation isn't about having all the answers—it's about keeping discussions structured, productive, and balanced.

One of the biggest challenges is managing strong personalities. Some people naturally dominate discussions, while others—often those with the most valuable insights—stay quiet.

I learned to redirect dominant voices by summarizing their points and then shifting to someone else:

- "That's a great insight. Let's hear from others—how does this impact your role?"

For those who stayed quiet, I started calling on them directly:

- "I'd love to hear your perspective, since you work with this process daily."

Keeping discussions focused is another challenge. If conversations start to drift, bring them back to the agenda:

- "This is a great discussion, but it's outside today's scope. Let's add it to the parking lot for future review."

Facilitation is about guiding, not controlling. When you create a structured but open environment, people feel comfortable contributing, and the best ideas surface.

Driving Decisions and Next Steps

A meeting without clear action items is just a conversation. Every discussion should end with:

- What was decided?
- Who is responsible for what?
- What's the deadline?

I used to assume that people would naturally follow through after a productive discussion. They won't. If there's no accountability, tasks get lost, and decisions stall.

To fix this, I started using a simple meeting wrap-up:

- "Here's what we decided today. John will follow up on X, Sarah will update Y, and we'll check in next Wednesday."

This small change ensured that discussions led to action, keeping projects on track and teams aligned.

Creating a Space for Collaboration

Facilitation is about more than just meetings—it's about creating an environment where teams work together effectively. When done well, people feel heard, projects stay on track, and decisions move forward.

The best facilitators aren't the ones who drive the meeting—they're the ones who guide the conversation and bring out the best in the group.

In the next chapter, we'll explore The Advocate role, where you'll learn how to balance innovation, usability, and safety while keeping patient-centered design at the heart of every decision.

Let's explore the next piece of the puzzle.

Practical Tips

Focus on guiding, not controlling.

- Great facilitators steer discussions rather than dominate them.
- Help the group reach conclusions organically instead of pushing decisions.

Create a structured but flexible environment.

- Set clear objectives before meetings so discussions stay on track.
- Be willing to adapt if the conversation leads to valuable insights.

Encourage all voices, not just the loudest ones.

- Call on quieter participants to ensure diverse perspectives are heard.
- Redirect dominating voices without shutting them down.

Clarify decisions and next steps before wrapping up.

- Summarize key takeaways and confirm action items with clear accountability.
- Ensure follow-ups happen so discussions lead to progress.

Facilitation isn't just about meetings—it's about fostering collaboration.

- Keep communication flowing between teams, not just during scheduled meetings.
- Use shared documents or project boards to track decisions and updates.

5

The Advocate—Finding Balance

Facilitation helps teams work together, but advocacy ensures that what's being built actually works for everyone involved. As an advocate, your job isn't just to speak up for one group of users—it's to ensure that solutions are designed with all impacted stakeholders in mind while still balancing safety, usability, and compliance.

One of the hardest lessons I learned was that people naturally advocate for themselves first. Clinicians think about their workflows, IT thinks about system constraints, leadership thinks about budgets and policies, and operations teams think about efficiency and reporting. Everyone sees the solution through their own lens, and few take the time to see how their decisions impact others across the organization—or the patient journey itself.

This is where advocacy becomes critical. You're not just representing one voice in the room—you're advocating for seamless workflows, cross-functional collaboration, and ultimately, the patient.

A perfect example of this was when we helped establish a new medication e-fill service for a large medical group—something that had never been done before. The program was physician-led, but the staff working in it weren't pharmacists. In order for them to be effective, they needed specific views, privileges, and workflows in the EHR to support providers in medication refill management.

The resistance to change was immediate. Because these staff weren't pharmacists, many stakeholders rejected the idea of giving them ordering privileges or anything that differed from the standard medical assistant role. We had to fight the assumption that existing EHR positions would be sufficient while doing everything possible to leverage what already existed before justifying the creation of something new.

This is where advocacy became crucial. We worked closely with compliance, physician leadership, pharmacy leadership, and IT—gathering evidence, mapping workflows, and negotiating every technical and policy decision from start to finish. The result? A brand-new EHR position that had never existed before, built specifically to meet the needs of this program while maintaining regulatory integrity.

This experience taught me that being an advocate means more than just voicing concerns—it means doing the technical and operational work to prove when a new solution is needed.

Where I Struggled

When I first stepped into the Advocate role, I thought my job was to make things easier for clinicians—to champion their requests and push for solutions that worked for them. But I quickly learned that advocacy isn't about fighting for one group—it's about finding solutions that work across the board. I struggled with three major challenges:

Overcoming resistance to change.

- Many stakeholders defaulted to "We've never done it that way before."
- The medication e-fill project faced significant pushback from those

who believed the standard medical assistant role should be sufficient.

Balancing usability, compliance, and safety.

- Just because a workflow made sense operationally didn't mean it fit within regulatory and compliance standards.
- We had to work closely with compliance teams to ensure we weren't creating unnecessary risk.

Proving when something new was necessary.

- Instead of jumping straight to building a new position, we first exhausted every possible option within the existing framework.
- It wasn't until we had technical proof that the standard role didn't work that we could successfully advocate for a new EHR position.

I found myself working with teams to think bigger—to move past their own role and see the impact of their choices on other clinicians, other departments, and most importantly, patients. It wasn't always easy, but it was necessary.

What I Learned

Advocacy isn't just about one group—it's about the bigger picture.

If I had only pushed for what the e-fill team wanted, we wouldn't have gained buy-in. Instead, I had to frame the request as part of a larger workflow solution that balanced provider, compliance, and operational needs.

Start by working within the system, then justify change.

Instead of demanding a new EHR position from the start, we first maximized existing roles. When those roles failed to meet the needs of the program, we had technical proof to support creating something new.

Collaboration is everything.

This project required engagement from compliance, pharmacy leadership, physician leadership, and IT. Without early engagement from all key stakeholders, this initiative would have failed.

Balancing Innovation and Compliance

One of the hardest parts of being an advocate is finding the right balance between innovation, usability, and compliance. Many times, users will request a feature or workflow change that makes perfect sense operationally, but when you look deeper, it doesn't align with security, safety, or regulatory requirements.

This doesn't mean that usability should take a backseat. It means that advocacy includes finding the right path forward—one that improves usability while meeting required standards.

During the medication e-fill project, we had to navigate these challenges firsthand. The e-fill team needed expanded EHR privileges, but granting them full ordering capabilities posed compliance risks. Instead of pushing back immediately, we worked with compliance teams to find creative solutions—leveraging existing security roles where possible and justifying the creation of new permissions where necessary.

Had we taken a hard line approach—either rejecting the request entirely or blindly supporting the provider team without considering compliance—this project would have failed. Instead, by staying engaged, offering alternatives, and backing up recommendations with evidence, we built something that worked for all stakeholders.

Advocacy isn't about always saying "yes" to user requests—it's about finding ways to say "yes" while keeping safety, security, and feasibility in mind.

Helping Teams See Beyond Their Own Perspective

One of the biggest challenges in advocacy is helping teams step outside their own role. Each stakeholder brings a specific perspective and set of priorities, but few naturally think about how their decisions impact others.

In the e-fill project, pharmacy leadership was focused on medication safety, compliance was focused on legal risk, and providers were focused on workflow efficiency. Each of these perspectives mattered—but they didn't naturally align with one another.

As an advocate, your job is to connect these perspectives and help teams see how their decisions impact others across the organization.

This often means asking the right questions:

- How does this impact the next step in the process?
- If we implement this change, will it create challenges for another team?
- What happens if this is rolled out at scale? Will it still work in every setting?

By encouraging teams to think beyond their own scope, you help them design solutions that work not just for them, but for the entire system.

Creating a Path Forward

Being an advocate doesn't mean pushing for the perfect solution—it means ensuring that the best possible solution is implemented within real-world constraints. Advocacy is about negotiating trade-offs, aligning competing priorities, and ensuring that patient-centered design remains at the heart of every decision.

In the medication e-fill project, this meant building a solution that was clinically sound, operationally efficient, and regulatory-compliant. We didn't get there overnight. It took iterations, negotiations, and testing before we reached a model that worked for everyone involved.

That's what advocacy looks like in practice—it's not just championing user requests or pushing for what seems easiest. It's working through the complexity, finding a workable path, and making sure the right decision is made—not just the most convenient one.

Advocacy in Action

Being an advocate isn't about fighting for one group—it's about ensuring that solutions work across departments, meet compliance, and ultimately improve patient care. When teams focus too much on their own needs, bring them back to the bigger picture:

- "How does this impact the patient?"
- "Are we unintentionally creating silos?"
- "Can this scale across different settings without breaking the workflow?"

When you keep these questions at the center of every discussion, you help organizations move beyond quick fixes and build solutions that last.

In the next chapter, we'll explore the Liaison role, where you'll focus on connecting teams, breaking down silos, and ensuring collaboration across departments. While advocacy is about defending the right solutions, being a liaison is about bridging communication gaps to make implementation successful.

Now, let's take this a step further.

Practical Tips

Encourage teams to see the whole process.

- Ask: "What happens before and after this step?"
- Map out workflows to help visualize how information flows between departments and where breakdowns might occur.

Start within the system before requesting new solutions.

- Demonstrate that existing tools and roles have been exhausted before advocating for new ones.
- Use technical evidence rather than opinions to justify the need for change.

Balance usability and safety.

- If a request doesn't meet compliance, offer alternatives that improve usability without breaking policy.
- Engage compliance teams early to prevent last-minute roadblocks.

Advocate for patient-centered design.

- When teams focus too much on their own needs, ask: "How does this affect the patient?"
- Bring discussions back to seamless patient care, not just individual convenience.

6

The Liaison—Connecting Teams

One of the most underrated but essential roles of an informaticist is that of The Liaison—the person who ensures that different teams talk to each other, understand each other, and collaborate effectively.

Healthcare is naturally full of silos. Clinical teams focus on patient care, IT focuses on technical systems, compliance teams worry about regulatory risks, and operations focuses on efficiency and business goals. Each group is working toward the same ultimate mission—delivering quality care—but their day-to-day priorities don't always align. That's where you come in.

As a liaison, your job is to bridge communication gaps, align priorities, and ensure that solutions are built with input from all relevant stakeholders. This isn't just about helping teams collaborate better—it's about preventing costly mistakes, ensuring seamless workflows, and making sure no one is left out of critical decisions.

However, being a liaison doesn't mean carrying this responsibility alone. Leadership sponsorship, clinical champions, and engaged stakeholders are essential to making this role successful and sustainable. When we have strong leadership support, our work as liaisons becomes more about guiding and enabling collaboration, rather than feeling like we have to carry every responsibility on our shoulders.

A tendency that many informaticists struggle with—including myself—is the feeling that the success of an initiative depends entirely on us. But we are not the sole owners of success—we are facilitators within a team.

When clinical sponsorship is strong, the organization is better positioned to collaborate. When leadership actively supports our efforts, it frees us up to be a more relaxed and effective liaison—a resource rather than a single point of accountability.

Where I Struggled

When I first stepped into this role, I assumed collaboration happened naturally—that teams would automatically include the right people in discussions and that stakeholders would work together toward shared goals. That assumption was wrong.

Instead, I saw a pattern:

- Decisions were often made in isolation—one department would move forward on a project without consulting others who would be directly affected.
- IT would build a solution based on what one clinical group requested, only to find out later that it didn't work for nursing or another department.
- Compliance teams would push back on a change late in the process because they hadn't been involved from the beginning.
- Market leadership would implement changes differently across locations, creating inconsistencies in how workflows functioned.

And here's where I struggled the most: I felt personally responsible for fixing these gaps. I thought that if I just worked harder, if I just connected the right people, if I just facilitated the conversations the right way, I could make everything align. But I was wrong.

As much as healthcare informatics professionals are key players in fostering collaboration, the reality is that we cannot do this alone. If leadership isn't engaged, if clinical sponsors aren't backing the effort, our ability to break down silos will always be limited.

What I Learned

Silos won't fix themselves—you have to recognize and break them.

I learned that it's not enough to assume teams will collaborate—you have to actively step in and connect the dots between groups. If you notice that a major decision is being made without key stakeholders, speak up and bring those voices into the conversation.

You need leadership sponsorship to drive real change.

When senior leaders and clinical sponsors actively support cross-team collaboration, everything flows more easily. If leadership is engaged, teams take the liaison role more seriously and collaboration becomes more natural.

Liaison efforts should be shared, not carried alone.

My mistake was thinking that I had to be the one ensuring collaboration happened in every discussion. I learned to delegate, engage clinical champions, and rely on leadership support instead of trying to manage everything myself.

Managing Competing Priorities Across Departments

One of the most difficult parts of being a liaison is managing competing priorities between different departments. Every team thinks their needs should take precedence:

- Clinicians want fewer clicks and more efficiency.
- IT prioritizes security, stability, and scalability.
- Compliance wants strict policy adherence to reduce risk.
- Operations focuses on standardization and reporting.

These priorities don't always align, and if no one steps in to mediate, projects stall, frustrations build, and changes fail.

With strong clinical sponsorship and leadership buy-in, this job becomes easier. When leadership sets the expectation that all groups need to work together, teams become more receptive to finding balanced solutions instead of fighting for their individual priorities.

Bridging Gaps and Building Collaboration

Being a liaison isn't about forcing collaboration—it's about creating the conditions where collaboration naturally happens. It's about ensuring that the right people are talking to each other, that decisions aren't made in a vacuum, and that technology solutions truly work across the entire system. And most importantly—it's about knowing that you are not responsible for solving this alone.

With strong leadership, engaged stakeholders, and clear sponsorship, an informaticist can truly serve as a resource to the organization, rather than feeling solely responsible for success.

In the next chapter, we'll explore The Designer role, where you take everything you've learned from observing, translating, facilitating, and advocating—and start building real-world solutions that work.

Now that we've laid the foundation, let's dive deeper.

Practical Tips

Be proactive in identifying silos.

- If you notice that one team is making changes without engaging other impacted groups, step in and connect them.
- Ask: "Who else needs to be part of this conversation?"

Engage leadership early to ensure collaboration.

- If leadership makes cross-team collaboration a priority, your job as a liaison becomes easier.
- Without leadership support, your efforts may stall or be deprioritized.

Clarify ownership and accountability.

- Define who owns each part of the workflow, who makes decisions, and who needs to be informed.
- If leadership is aligned on this, it prevents confusion and delays later on.

Encourage clinical champions to advocate for change.

- If a provider-led initiative needs system-wide collaboration, engage respected clinical voices to help drive engagement.
- Peer-to-peer advocacy is often more effective than external pres-

sure from IT or informatics.

7

The Designer—Real-World Solutions

Designing workflows and system changes in informatics is deceptively complex. The best designs look simple to the end user, but behind the scenes, countless considerations, dependencies, and system interactions must be carefully thought through.

At first, I thought designing a new form or adding a field was straightforward—just place it where users need it and move on. But I quickly learned that every single design decision has downstream effects, and failing to account for them leads to frustration, rework, and broken workflows. Let's take a simple example: Adding a new field to a form.

- Does this field need to be included in reports?
- Will it impact decision support rules or alerting?
- Does it need to be visible in other areas of the chart?
- Does this information need to be shared externally through a Health Information Exchange (HIE)?
- Will this field be available to patients in the patient portal?

What seems like a minor change can actually require a major design review to ensure system integrity. If you don't catch these details during the design phase, they'll catch up with you later—when reports fail, alerts misfire, or patient data is incomplete.

Design is a Collaborative Effort—Not a Solo Decision

As an informaticist, we don't approve design changes. Our role is to thoughtfully create designs in collaboration with stakeholders, prepare them for governance review, and ensure they are complete before approval.

If your organization doesn't have a formal governance process, it's important to establish a reliable review and signoff structure. Designs should always be reviewed by the right stakeholders before implementation, ensuring they are well-thought-out and aligned with clinical, operational, and technical priorities.

In this chapter, we'll explore:

- Best practices for structuring new electronic documentation elements
- How to evaluate existing designs before making changes
- Strategies for testing and refining design decisions before governance review

Where I Struggled

Early in my career, I thought designing system changes was about implementing what the user asked for. If a provider requested a new form or an additional field, I thought my job was to make it happen. But I quickly realized that design isn't about taking requests—it's about evaluating the full impact of a change. I struggled with three major challenges:

Underestimating the complexity of system design.

- I didn't initially realize how one change could break multiple downstream workflows.
- A field added to a form wasn't just a field on a form—it had to be mapped correctly for reporting, considered for visibility in the patient portal, and integrated properly with existing workflows.

Failing to engage the right technical resources early.

- I would start designing without fully understanding how the system functioned behind the scenes.
- Analysts and IT teams had critical insights about data structures, system rules, and existing configurations—but I wasn't pulling them into conversations soon enough.

Assuming design decisions were final once built.

- I used to think once something was designed and implemented, it was done. But I quickly learned that good design requires iteration and governance review before approval.
- I had to shift from "build it and move on" to "refine, validate, and prepare for review."

Best Practices for Structuring New Electronic Documentation Elements

One of the most frequent design requests in informatics is adding new electronic documentation elements—whether it's a new form, a new data field, a revised template, an updated flowsheet, or changes to clinical documentation workflows. It sounds simple, but getting it right requires deep system awareness, structured decision-making, and careful alignment with clinical needs.

Key Considerations for New Documentation Elements

Before designing, I always ask:

- Where will this documentation live in the patient chart?
- Does it need to be easily accessible across multiple roles, or is it specific to a particular user group?
- Will this data need to flow into other sections of the chart, such as summaries, reports, or decision support tools?
- Does this require integration with other applications (e.g., HIE feeds, patient portals, billing, quality reporting)?
- Will this impact note templates, structured documentation, or clinical alerts?
- Does this replace an existing documentation element, or is it truly adding something new?

Avoiding Documentation Bloat and Form Overload

A major challenge in informatics is preventing documentation bloat. Over time, EMRs tend to accumulate redundant or outdated documentation elements, leading to clutter, confusion, and inefficiencies.

Before creating a new element, consider:

- Can an existing template, form, or flowsheet be modified to meet this need?
- Is this request duplicating information already captured elsewhere?
- Will this introduce unnecessary documentation burdens, making workflows more complex rather than more efficient?

A well-designed documentation element doesn't just store data—it enhances workflow efficiency, supports patient care, and ensures accurate, retrievable information.

Strategies for Testing and Refining Design Decisions Before Governance Review

Governance committees expect well-thought-out, validated designs, not unfinished concepts. A good pre-governance design review should include:

- A technical check—does this design align with system best practices?
- A clinical workflow validation—does this change make sense from a usability perspective?
- A compliance review—does this change introduce any regulatory concerns?

Testing in a lower environment is essential. A design that looks great on paper may have unexpected issues when built into the system. By catching these before governance review, the final approval process goes much more smoothly.

Final Thoughts on Design Review and Governance

Good design is intentional, collaborative, and iterative. It's about thoughtfully structuring changes, testing assumptions, and ensuring stakeholder alignment before moving forward.

Most importantly, we don't make these decisions alone—design must go through structured review, stakeholder engagement, and governance approval before implementation.

In the next chapter, we'll explore The Change Manager role, where we take approved designs and focus on successful implementation, user adoption, and training.

We're not done yet—let's keep building.

Practical Tips

Start with the End in Mind

- Define the problem you're solving before designing anything.
- Clarify what success looks like—how will you know if the solution works?

Build in Layers—Iterate and Refine

- Don't try to solve everything at once. Start with the foundation, test it, and build on it.
- Think of it like constructing a house—you wouldn't put the roof on before the walls.

Validate Designs with End Users

- Test real world working scenarios before go-live.
- Shadow users and observe how they interact with the new process.
- Gather feedback and adjust as needed.

Simplify Every Step

- Every extra step or click increases frustration.
- Ask: Does this step really need to be here?
- Ask: Can this process be automated?
- Ask: Is there a simpler way to achieve the same result?

Ensure System Integrity

- Ask: Does this field need to be included in reports?
- Ask: Will it impact decision support rules or alerts?
- Ask: Does it need to be visible in other areas of the chart?

Review and Approve at Every Step

- Engage stakeholders in governance review before implementation.
- Ensure regulatory, clinical, and technical teams sign off before deployment.

Document Everything Clearly

- Use plain language—technical teams need clear requirements, not vague requests.
- Provide workflow diagrams or screenshots to align expectations.

Test in Lower Environments First

- Use non-production domains or test patients to simulate real workflows.
- Verify that every interaction works before implementation.

Plan for Adoption and Training

- The best design is useless if no one knows how to use it.
- Ensure training materials and support are available before go-live.
- Create training material from the perspective of the position using the enhancement. It needs to make sense to their workflow

Be Ready to Adjust

- It's more common than you think to realize a "miss" when taking a change to production. Be open to iterating based on real-world use.
- Gather feedback post-implementation and make necessary refinements.

8

The Change Manager—Shepherding Governance

Informatics is filled with ideas, complaints, and requests for change. Some come from frontline staff who see inefficiencies firsthand. Others stem from regulatory requirements or leadership initiatives. Regardless of the source, one hard-earned lesson I've learned is that we should never charge forward on a complaint or suggestion without first doing the necessary pre-work.

Governance Starts Before a Request Becomes a Project

Good governance doesn't start at a formal review meeting—it starts long before that, in the early stages of defining the problem. Before an idea moves forward, I ask:

- Is this truly new content, or does a version of it already exist somewhere?
- Is this driven by a regulatory requirement, operational efficiency, or user frustration?
- If it's regulatory, do we already document this in another way?

- If it's a request for efficiency, is it solving a real problem, or is there a workaround that's already working?
- If it's fixing something broken, what is the root cause?

Too often, people request a build change before clearly defining the actual problem. I've seen many well-intended requests turn into unnecessary work because no one took the time to ask, "Is this truly needed?"

The pre-governance phase is about problem definition, leadership sponsorship, and strategic prioritization—because no organization can act on every request at once.

Leadership Sets the Priorities—Not Us

Another critical lesson I've learned is that an informaticist is not the decision-maker. We are the shepherds of change management, guiding requests through a structured process—but leadership sets the priorities.

It's tempting to push forward with changes that seem logical or urgent, but not everything is a top priority. That's why seeking sponsorship and leadership support upfront is so critical. Leadership helps define:

- Where this request fits within the organization's strategic priorities.
- Whether other projects already in flight take precedence.
- Whether this is a problem worth solving now—or if it can wait.

If leadership isn't engaged from the start, a healthcare informatics professional risks pushing forward on something that ultimately won't get approved—wasting time and resources.

Governance is Not Just a Sign-Off Process—It's a Safeguard

On the other end of the spectrum, once a request has been validated, prioritized, and developed into a well-thought-out design, it should never be approved for build without structured review and signoff.

This is especially true for anything outside standard system maintenance. Governance exists for a reason:

- To ensure that changes align with organizational goals.
- To prevent unintended consequences from poor design choices.
- To engage the right stakeholders before implementation.

I've seen cases where well-intended but unvetted changes were rushed into production—only to cause more harm than good. A broken report, a workflow that inadvertently hid critical patient data, or an unnecessary documentation requirement that added more burden without improving care.

This is why change management requires discipline. Just because a request has merit doesn't mean it should go forward without careful review.

Pre-Governance: Define the Problem Before Proposing a Solution

A good governance process starts before a request even reaches the formal review stage. This means clearly defining the problem before jumping to design.

Key questions to ask before moving forward:

- What is the actual issue or opportunity?
- What are we trying to fix, improve, or comply with?

- Is there existing documentation or workflow that already captures part of this need?
- Who is impacted by this change?
- Who needs to sponsor this request at the leadership level?

Many times, frontline teams request system changes that could actually be addressed through better training or workflow adjustments rather than a technical build. This step helps prevent unnecessary system changes.

Prioritization: Engaging Leadership to Align Workload

Once a request is validated as necessary, the next step is to align it with the organization's priorities. Even great ideas may not be the most important thing to tackle right now. Leadership sponsorship ensures:

- The request fits within active strategic initiatives.
- Other high-priority projects aren't impacted by competing resources.
- There is clear accountability for decision-making.

If leadership isn't engaged in prioritization, informaticists risk over-promising and under-delivering.

Governance Review: A Formal Checkpoint Before Build Approval

A governance committee isn't just a rubber stamp—it serves as a final validation before system changes are built and implemented.

A strong governance review includes:

- Clinical validation—Does this change make sense from a workflow and patient safety perspective?

- Technical review—Is the design built in alignment with best practices and system integrity?
- Compliance check—Does this change create any regulatory or security risks?

This step ensures that what gets built is necessary, well-designed, and ready for adoption.

Final Thoughts on Change Management

Change management isn't just about getting changes built and implemented—it's about guiding them through a structured, thoughtful process that ensures success.

At every stage—problem definition, prioritization, governance review, and implementation—the informaticist plays the role of a shepherd, not the final decision-maker.

In the next chapter, we'll explore the Student role, where we shift focus from leading change to continuous learning, staying ahead of industry trends, and growing as an informaticist.

Onward—we have more to uncover.

Practical Tips

Never start with a solution—always define the problem first.

- If the problem isn't clearly defined, don't move forward.
- Engage clinical and operational stakeholders to validate the issue before working on a fix.

Ensure leadership sponsorship before moving forward.

- If leadership isn't engaged, the request may not be a priority.
- Work with leadership teams to align the change with active initiatives.

Establish a structured review process before implementation.

- Governance isn't about slowing things down—it's about making sure good changes move forward the right way.
- If governance doesn't exist, advocate for a structured approval process to prevent chaos.

Change is more than just system updates—it's about adoption.

- Once a change is approved, ensure there is a clear communication and training plan for users.
- If end users don't understand the change, they won't adopt it.

9

The Student—Embracing The Journey

One of the biggest surprises in my informatics career was realizing that learning never stops. No matter how much experience I gained, how many workflows I optimized, or how many governance processes I helped establish, there was always more to learn. The field of clinical informatics doesn't stand still. Technology evolves. Regulations shift. Organizational priorities change. Just when I think I have a system figured out, something new emerges that forces me to step back, reassess, and approach the situation with fresh eyes.

That's been the biggest lesson: Even with experience, I still go back to the basics.

Early in my career, I thought that eventually, I would reach a point where I had it all figured out—where my accumulated knowledge would allow me to confidently approach any request or problem without hesitation. But over time, my greatest realization wasn't that I don't know enough—it was that the best way to approach informatics is to assume I don't know.

I call this my "fresh eyes" perspective—walking into every situation as if I were encountering it for the first time, asking basic questions, and ensuring I truly understand what's happening before making assumptions. Even when I've handled similar situations a dozen times before, I step through the workflow, observe it like a first-time user, and ask questions that might seem overly simplistic—on purpose.

Some of the biggest mistakes in informatics happen not because we lack knowledge, but because we assume too much. The way something worked last year—or even last month—might not be how it works today. A regulatory change, a system upgrade, or a small tweak to a third-party integration can shift a workflow in ways that aren't immediately obvious. The only way to catch those changes before they cause issues is to approach every situation as a student—curious, methodical, and unwilling to rely on assumptions.

The same applies to learning the technology itself. With each system upgrade, new functionality is introduced. Third-party vendors are integrated. Legacy features are deprecated. Informatics isn't just about knowing workflows—it's about staying engaged with the tools that support them.

Being a student in informatics isn't about formal training programs or certifications—though those have their place. It's about developing a mindset of continuous learning—always observing, always stepping through workflows, and always asking "What's changed?"

Where I Struggled

Early in my career, I thought that experience would eventually lead to mastery—that at some point, I would have enough knowledge to confidently handle any informatics challenge that came my way. I believed that if I could just learn enough about system design, workflows, governance, and clinical best practices, I would finally reach a point where I had it all figured out.

But instead of reaching a moment where I could say, "I know everything I need to know", I realized something even more valuable: The best way to maintain expertise is to assume I don't know.

Rather than relying on what I think I know, I now approach every change, every upgrade, and every workflow review as if I were seeing it for the first time. I ask basic, almost obvious questions:

- What exactly is happening at each step?
- Has anything changed since the last time I worked on this?
- Is there an assumption here that hasn't been verified?

This was a major shift for me. Instead of feeling pressure to already have the answers, I learned to focus on asking the right questions.

At first, I struggled with the idea of going back to the basics, especially after years of experience. I worried that people might wonder why I was asking fundamental questions about workflows I had seen before. But then I realized that this is exactly what keeps mistakes from happening.

Another challenge was keeping up with constant changes in technology. Each system upgrade introduced new functionality. We integrated third-party vendors that altered workflows. Small tweaks in backend system configurations sometimes caused downstream effects we didn't anticipate. I quickly learned that technical literacy is just as important as workflow knowledge. If I didn't actively engage with IT analysts and explore the system myself, I would eventually fall behind.

I also learned that even a tiny change can have a big impact. A new field added to a form isn't just a new field—it could affect reporting, decision support, or even interoperability with external systems. If I only looked at changes from the surface level, I risked missing critical downstream effects.

What I Learned

The best way to avoid mistakes is to act like I don't know—every time.

Even when I'm familiar with a workflow, I walk through it as if I'm new to it. I don't rely on memory alone—I step through the system, ask basic questions, and verify every assumption.

Staying ahead means learning, relearning, and learning again.

The system today isn't the same system it was six months ago. I have to stay engaged with system updates, new vendor tools, and back-end configurations to make informed decisions.

Asking basic questions prevents major design flaws.

It's not about what I assume—I need to ask end users what they're actually doing, observe them in real-time, and test the process myself. The things that seem obvious are often the ones that get overlooked.

Technical knowledge is critical—but relationships are how you learn it.

I've learned more from sitting with IT analysts, application managers, and back-end system experts than from reading any documentation. Developing strong relationships with technical teams helps bridge the gap between clinical requests and system capabilities.

The Value of Mentorship and Networking in Informatics Growth

One of the most valuable things I've done in my career is building relationships with people who challenge me, support me, and teach me what I don't know.

Early on, I relied too much on figuring things out myself. I didn't want to admit when I didn't understand something, and I assumed I could just research my way to an answer. But informatics is a people-driven field. The more I connected with experienced informaticists, IT analysts, and clinical leaders, the more I realized that mentorship and networking are the fastest ways to grow.

A good mentor doesn't just answer questions—they challenge your thinking. Some of the best mentors I've had would push me to consider:

- "Are you solving the right problem?"
- "Who else should be involved in this conversation?"
- "What are the downstream effects of this change?"

These weren't answers I could have found in a textbook or training module. They were insights gained from experience, and mentorship gave me access to that knowledge without having to learn everything the hard way.

When you have a good mentor, let me tell you that even well after you part ways, they will always be with you, helping to craft the next great thing you do. For me, I am eternally grateful for Dr. Robert Weber, Dr. Steven Magee, Terri Wilson, and Lori Nelson. Without all of these amazing people (and even more than these), I wouldn't be where I am today.

Networking also played a huge role in my growth. Whether through conferences, informatics groups, or internal professional circles, having trusted peers to exchange ideas with has been invaluable. Sometimes, the best way to find a solution is to ask, "Has anyone else dealt with this before?" The informatics community is full of people willing to share what they've learned, and tapping into that knowledge can save time, effort, and frustration.

Mentorship and networking aren't about career advancement alone—they're about becoming better at the work itself. Surrounding yourself with people who understand the challenges, who see things differently, and who have been through similar experiences makes you a better informaticist.

How Continuous Learning Strengthens Problem-Solving and Decision-Making

Informatics is full of gray areas. Unlike clinical practice, where many decisions are based on clear protocols, healthcare technology requires balancing competing priorities, working through uncertainty, and making judgment calls in complex situations.

The more I commit to learning, the better I become at solving problems. Every time I go through a new system upgrade, a major workflow redesign, or a governance review process, I build on what I've learned before. Over time, I started recognizing patterns, anticipating challenges, and asking better questions upfront.

Continuous learning has also made me more confident in decision-making. In the past, I hesitated, second-guessed myself, and felt unsure about whether I was making the right call. But the more I invested in learning, the more I developed an internal knowledge bank to draw from—not just technical knowledge, but experience-based intuition.

That said, experience alone isn't enough. Healthcare technology is evolving faster than ever. AI is becoming integrated into decision support tools, interoperability is expanding, and automation is reshaping workflows. If I stopped learning today, I'd be behind in just a few months.

The best informaticists aren't the ones with the most years of experience—they're the ones who stay engaged, stay curious, and never assume they know it all.

Final Thoughts Before Moving Forward

Being a Student in informatics isn't about learning for the sake of learning—it's about becoming more effective, more adaptable, and more confident in navigating change.

In the next sections of this chapter, we'll explore:

- How to stay ahead of industry trends without getting overwhelmed.
- The value of mentorship and networking in informatics growth.
- How continuous learning strengthens problem-solving and decision-making.

Let's go wrap things up.

Practical Tips

Never assume. Always walk through the process.

- Even if I've seen the workflow before, I step through it again from start to finish.
- I approach changes with a "captain obvious" mindset—verifying every detail, no matter how basic it seems.

Stay engaged with system updates.

- EHR upgrades, third-party integrations, and back-end changes all impact workflows.
- Keeping up with technical advancements is just as important as understanding workflows.

Ask the simplest questions to avoid the biggest mistakes.

- "Has this changed?"
- "Who else touches this process?"
- "Is there something we're assuming that we haven't tested?"

Invest time in technical learning.

- Spend time with IT and analysts to understand how the system works behind the scenes.
- Learning how data moves through the system makes for better, more informed design decisions.

10

Conclusion

This book has been about the many roles an informaticist plays—the Observer, the Translator, the Facilitator, the Advocate, the Liaison, the Designer, the Change Manager, and the Student.

Each of these roles builds on the next. Together, they define the real-world experience of working in informatics—not just the technical skills, but the mindset, the problem-solving, and the ability to navigate a complex, ever-changing landscape.

But more than anything, this book is about helping others succeed in informatics. Whether you're just starting your career or you've been doing this work for years, my hope is that this book has helped you recognize your own strengths, avoid common pitfalls, and approach this field with confidence and curiosity.

Because at the end of the day, that's what informatics is all about:

✔ Solving real problems that impact patient care.
✔ Bridging the gap between technology and clinical workflows.
✔ Helping organizations make smart, strategic decisions.
✔ And constantly learning, growing, and improving.

The work isn't always easy. It isn't always predictable. But it's worth it.

Let's keep learning. Let's keep improving. Let's keep making healthcare technology better for everyone who uses it.

Made in the USA
Monee, IL
04 November 2026

67384809R00046